actors'
workshop

Cameron and Margaret Yerian, Editors

 CHILDRENS PRESS, CHICAGO

Executive Editors
Cameron John Yerian, M.A.
Margaret A. Yerian, M.A.

Art Director
Thomas Petiet, M.F.A.

Designer
Cameron John Yerian

Senior Editors
Mary Rush, M.F.A.
Sharon Irvine, B.A.
Susan Keezer

Contributors
Nancy Muhlbach, M.A.
Jerry Gillmore, B.A.
Mary White, B.A.
Edith Wolter, B.S.
Virginia Foster, A.B.

Editorial Assistant
Phoebe A. Yerian

Readability Consultants
Donald E.P. Smith, Ph.D.
School of Education
University of Michigan

Judith K. Smith, Ph.D.
University of Michigan

Instructional Development Consultant
Joel B. Fleming, M.A.
Instructional Development & Technology
Michigan State University

Synectics Consultant
Gershom Clark Morningstar, M.A.
President, Wolverine-Morningstar Media

Art Consultant
Doris A. Smith, M.S.
Associate Professor of Art & Design
Eastern Michigan University

Library Consultant
Noel Winkler M.A.L.S.
Lecturer, Children's Literature
University of Michigan

Library of Congress Cataloging in Publication Data

Yerian, Cameron John.
  Actors' workshop.

  "Fun time books."
  SUMMARY: Text and illustrations present activities
designed to teach the basic techniques of acting and
the use of the imagination.
  1. Acting—Juvenile literature. [1. Acting]
I. Yerian, Margaret, joint author. II. Title.
PN2061.Y47   792'.028   74-12448
ISBN 0-516-01307-6

Contents

ACTING 5

Acting Alone 6
More than One 8
Echoes 10
Shadows 11
Silly Situations 12
An Awful Muddle 14
I Can't Hear You! 16
Acting Workshop 18

MOVE IT 21

Get Loose 22
Shake Down 24
Walk-About 25
Ocean Motion 26
Kitchen Action 28
Springs & Things 30
Grab Box 32
A Little Music, Please 34
Off the Record 36

ALL MIME 37

Scents & Nonsense 38
Change Is Strange 40
Silence Is Golden 42
Pass It On 43
Got the Picture? 44
Guess Again 46

INDEX 47

ACTORS' WORKSHOP

Enter the fascinating world of actors and acting. Make believe you are Little Red Riding Hood, the evil wolf, or an ocean wave. How would you act if you were . . . a toaster . . . a mad man . . . a whale? Pretend you can't speak and explore the world of pantomime, using your body movements and facial expression to tell your story. Act by yourself . . . or with your friends. Act out a silly situation, a dramatic event, or a scary play.

All these activities, and many more, are included in this book. Acting is fun. Don't hold back. Be free. Really be the character or thing you are imitating. You want your audience to really believe you and get involved with the story you are telling.

You don't need props or costumes all the time. But sometimes they add realism to a performance. Decide for yourself how much of your story will be told with props and how much can be told just using your imagination.

Write your own play or select a play from the library. Pick your actors. Organize your props. Practice . . . practice . . . practice. Then put on a performance for your friends and their parents.

Here are a few hints to get your Actors' Workshop organized.

- Have a special place for practice and prop storage.
- Plan what exercises and make believe activities you will do.
- Encourage your friends to try out for parts.
- Put on a public performance. This will keep your actors interested.
- Practice! The harder you work, the better the performance.

Let your creative self go. You are the actor. Don't get embarrassed or discouraged. If you and your fellow actors practice, you will have fun and so will your audience.

HAVE FUN WITH THE FUN TIME BOOKS

Acting Alone

STAND in front of a mirror. Count to 25 in a witch's voice. Show how mean she is using your voice. Do not move any part of your body.

PRETEND you are a very sad baby. Use your eyes and face only. No voice, please.

SHOW someone asking for something. Use your face and hands. Do not talk.

If you feel a giggle coming on, let it out. Then go back and try again without giggling.

FACE the mirror. Think about the story of Red Riding Hood.

PRETEND you are Red Riding Hood when she first sees the wolf in the forest. Is she afraid?

PRETEND you are the wolf. He has just seen Red Riding Hood in the forest. How does he look when he is thinking about getting to Grandmother's house?

WALK AWAY from the mirror. Skip to the mirror the way you think Red Riding Hood might skip. Skip away.

SNEAK BACK to the mirror the way that sneaky wolf got to Grandmother's house. The rascal.

More than One

PRETEND you are visiting another country. You can't speak its language. Ask a friend to be a store owner. Try to buy things from him. Perhaps birdseed, gloves, and film for your camera.

USE hand motions to show what you want. Your friend pretends he doesn't understand you.

PAY the store owner. Did you give him the right amount of money? He might have to make change.

GET the kids together. Sit in a circle. You start the action. *No speaking.*

USE your hands to pretend to be making or doing something. You might want to make a pie. Or lead a band. You decide. The first person who guesses what you are doing gets the next turn.

KEEP it going until everyone has had a turn. Try to think of harder things to do.

TEAM UP in twos or threes. Each team can perform for the others. A team needs more space and could stand up rather than sit. One team could be circus ponies. Or a pack of lonely coyotes. Hibernating bears?

Sh.

Echoes

FIND a partner and a newspaper.

READ a sentence from the newspaper out loud. Ask your partner to repeat it just the way you read it. He should use the same kind of voice you used. How closely can he copy your voice?

GIVE the newspaper to your friend. Let him read a sentence to you. Can you repeat it using the same kind of voice?

Since you have the newspaper open, act out your favorite comic strip.

FOLD the newspaper and put it away.

10

Shadows

FACE your friend standing up. Pretend you are getting ready to go ice-skating. Your friend is your shadow. He must do everything you do. He has to move the way you do. Put on warm clothes and your skating hat and mittens. Don't forget your skates. Is the shadow ready to go?

SWITCH places. Now pretend you are at the skating rink. Your friend is the skater. You are the shadow. Copy the skater's motions.

If the shadow falls down and the skater is still skating, something is wrong.

11

SiLLY SiTUaTiONS

ASK friends to pretend they are in a swimming class. This is the first day, and they are afraid of the water. You are the swimming teacher.

TALK the class into getting into the water. They will not. Some of them cry. Some try to leave. Some get angry. Keep trying to get them into the water. Tell them how much fun they will have.

CHANGE PLACES.

PRETEND you are the only one in the swimming class. You will not get into the water.

ASK one friend to pretend to be your mother. Another can be the teacher. Another can be your big brother. Do you have a sister?

ACT scared. They will try to talk you into getting into the pool.

GIVE IN. All of you pretend to swim.

An Awful Muddle

ASK your friends to act out an animal parade.

CHOOSE a leader. Pick kids to be geese, cats, rabbits, frogs, dogs, mice, lambs and snakes. Other kids can be owners.

MAKE some mistakes in lining them up. Put the cats behind the mice. The geese might tease the frogs—let them march together. Dogs chase rabbits. Might a snake want to get close to a lamb to stay warm?

MARCH AROUND. The animals must do what the owners want them to.

14

PRETEND a truck dumps a load of feathers on your parade. Animals and owners get mixed up. The sneezing is a help—it gets rid of some feathers.

ADD a friend to be a policeman. He thinks your parade made the feather mess. He wants it cleaned up NOW. You all try to tell him those are not your feathers. He will not listen.

CLEAN UP the mess—you are good citizens.

TAKE the parade home. You have worked hard.

The snakes never picked up one feather.

I Can't Hear You!

GET a telephone book and a friend.

STAND back to back with the friend. Read one name and telephone number from the book. The friend should repeat the name and number.

TAKE three big steps away from your friend. He should do the same. Read the next name and number. The friend repeats.

KEEP WALKING away from each other, reading and repeating. How far can you go and still hear each other without screaming?

Would you like to try the yellow pages?

SAY the word "look" in as many ways as you can. Whisper it, shout it, laugh it out. Say "look" in a nasty voice and then in a nice voice. Pretend you are asking a question with the word "look."

READ this out loud:
"Turn left at the cabbage." Now read it three more times. Make "turn" stand out, then "left," and then "cabbage" as you read.

    Turn left at the cabbage. (Don't go straight ahead.)

    Turn *left* at the cabbage. (Not right.)

    Turn left at the *cabbage*. (Not at the turnip.)

TRY other sentences, making your voice change the meaning in an idea.

Acting Workshop

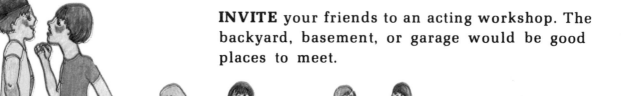

INVITE your friends to an acting workshop. The backyard, basement, or garage would be good places to meet.

MAKE UP some situations for acting practice. Pick one person to be a baseball umpire. Another person can be first baseman. Choose a batter. The batter argues with the first baseman and umpire. Is he safe or out at first base? The rest of the group can join in as fans. Each person should pick a side to agree with. Let everyone argue for a few minutes. Time out!

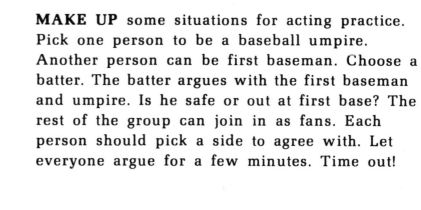

CHOOSE someone to pretend to be a mother. Pick a child from the group and get someone to pretend to be a lost dog. The child wants to keep the dog. The mother doesn't want it. The child tries to get Mom to let him keep the dog. Mother is stern. The child wants the dog. The dog begs to stay.

ASK each friend to think of a story or play he likes. Act out each one. Use as many actors as you can. Pick different kinds of stories so each person can play a mean, happy, or funny part.

USE your own words in acting out the story.

THINK about the part you are playing. Make it as real as you can using your voice and different motions.

In a workshop, you don't need real furniture. If the story calls for a table, use a box. Three chairs can be lined up to make a sofa.

Sylvester and the Magic Pebble would be fun to do in your workshop. You can get this book from the library.

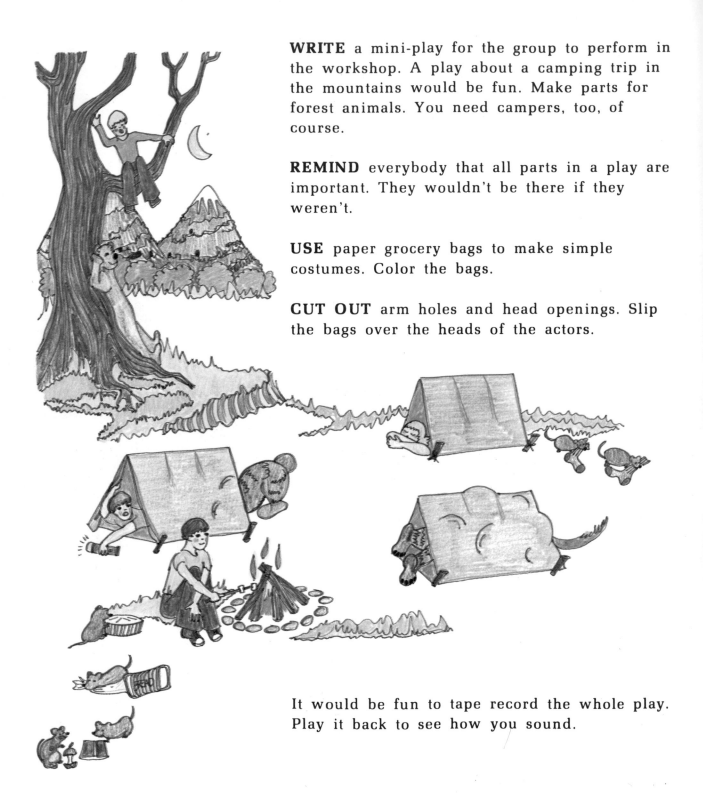

WRITE a mini-play for the group to perform in the workshop. A play about a camping trip in the mountains would be fun. Make parts for forest animals. You need campers, too, of course.

REMIND everybody that all parts in a play are important. They wouldn't be there if they weren't.

USE paper grocery bags to make simple costumes. Color the bags.

CUT OUT arm holes and head openings. Slip the bags over the heads of the actors.

It would be fun to tape record the whole play. Play it back to see how you sound.

GeT LOoSe

STAND as still and as straight as you can. Pretend you are a board. How long can you stay that way? It isn't much fun. Let's relax and get into a moving mood.

WEAR your favorite play clothes. If you can swing a ball bat or kick a can in them, they fit just right. Perhaps you would rather wear your swimsuit. Bare feet would be nice. Too cold? Then put on your gym shoes.

GET your gang together for a creeping race.

FIND a room or space big enough for all of you. Go outside if you can.

LINE everybody up on their hands and knees. You stand seven giant steps from the line. When you yell "GO" the racers creep to you then creep *backward* to the starting line. The winner is the one who doesn't fall down.

Shake Down

STRETCH your arms as high above your head as you can. Stand on your tiptoes. Wiggle your fingers as fast as you can. Now your hands, then arms. Keep wiggling until your whole body is moving.

PRETEND you are a puppet. The puppet is very upset. He got on the wrong plane and flew to Alaska. He has no coat. He is shivering and shaking.

SHIVER and SHAKE your way to the floor and back up again.

STOP shaking and rest.

24

Walk-About

WALK across the room. Now walk back like your mother walks in the morning. Walk like the meanest person you know.

PRETEND you are carrying a big load of bricks on your back. Walk 20 steps. Unload those bricks and walk back.

THINK about how you would walk if someone were pulling you. You don't want to go in that direction. How would you walk?

SHOW your mother how you would walk if you were going to the store to buy ice cream. Or spinach.

Ocean Motion

INVITE some kids to join you in slow motion.

SIT on the floor. Move your arms and body like ocean waves on a calm day. If a storm comes up, the waves will get higher and stronger.

STAND UP. Pretend you are seaweed floating around in the water. Some floats in place. Some floats away.

SIT cross-legged on the floor. Bend forward and wrap your arms around your legs. Pretend you are giant clams opening and closing.

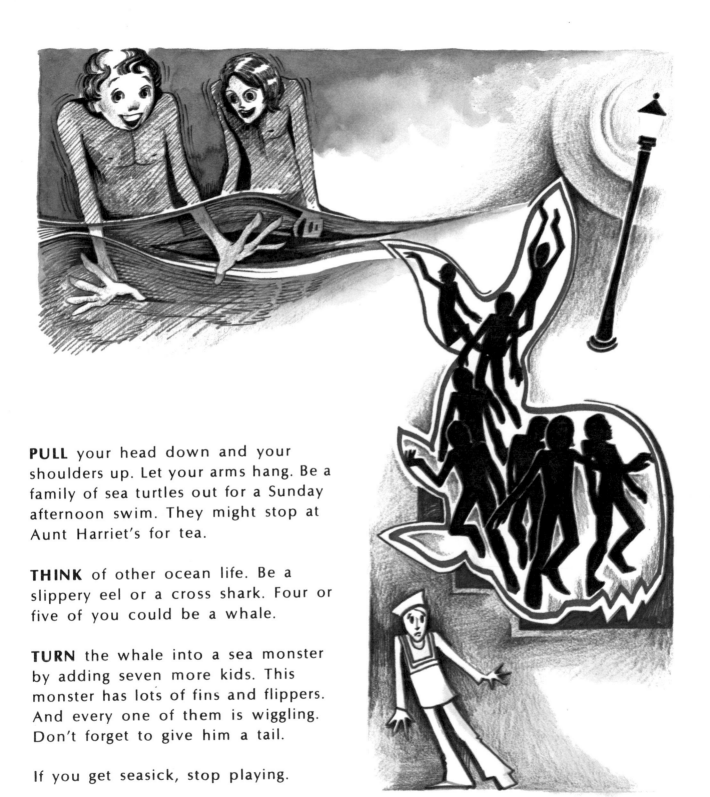

PULL your head down and your shoulders up. Let your arms hang. Be a family of sea turtles out for a Sunday afternoon swim. They might stop at Aunt Harriet's for tea.

THINK of other ocean life. Be a slippery eel or a cross shark. Four or five of you could be a whale.

TURN the whale into a sea monster by adding seven more kids. This monster has lots of fins and flippers. And every one of them is wiggling. Don't forget to give him a tail.

If you get seasick, stop playing.

27

Kitchen Action

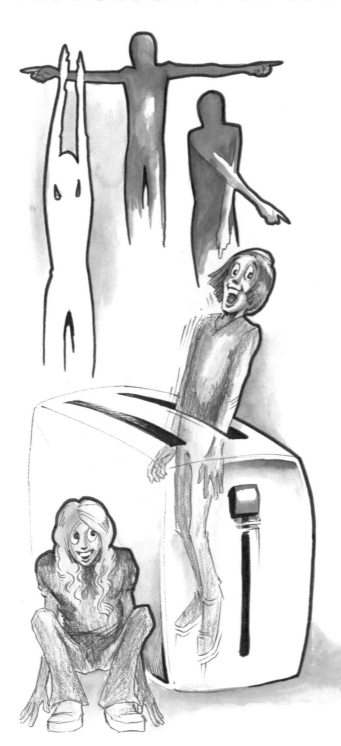

GO into the kitchen. What do you see? A toaster? A mixer? Curtains?

LOOK at the clock. Stand straight and pretend your arms are the hands on that clock. Can your arms show the time? Make them show 12:00, 4:30, and 9:15.

SIT on the floor. Pretend you are bread in the toaster. Count to ten slowly and pop up! With a friend, make enough toast to go with six cups of cocoa.

PRETEND you are the potato masher.

28

MAKE a circle on the floor with about 10 feet of string. Stand in the circle with a friend.

PRETEND you are the beaters in a mixer. Use your arms and legs. Turn together slowly if you are mixing thick batter. Move quickly if you are beating eggs.

GET lots of kids sitting down together on the floor. Pretend you are popcorn being popped.

HOLD HANDS with two other people. Close your eyes and move slowly like curtains blowing in a breeze.

Springs & Things

PRETEND you are a very tiny spring. Bounce from your bedroom to the kitchen. Now you are a big spring. You can go farther and make bigger leaps. Go out of doors and spring around the house.

PUT your hands on your hips. Right foot in front of left foot, please. Try to slide your right foot forward and your left foot back at the same time. Now bring them together quickly. Do it three more times. You just took your first scissors steps.

SHAKE your legs if they feel tired.

THINK about the windshield wipers on a car. You can make the same movement. Stand up. Keep your arms straight and move them in the same way the wipers move in a gentle rain. The wipers work harder and faster in a heavy rain.

PRETEND you are something in your mom's washing machine. Put your hands on your chest, elbows straight out. Twist back and forth. Try to go up and down while you twist. Stop. The washing is done. Now spin, spin, spin. That gets all the water out.

Grab Box

FIND a large box. Is it empty? Good.

FILL the box with different things: a feather, scarf, man's hat, walking cane, bottle, book, ruler, towel, and anything else you can think of.

FIND a broom, small chair, footstool, and clothes basket. Put these things in a pile next to the box.

GET some friends together. Add some kids you don't know very well.

TAKE TURNS. Go to the box and pick out one thing. Or choose something from the pile.

MAKE UP a short dance using the thing you chose. If the feather makes you think of a chicken, do a chicken dance. The towel could be wrapped around your head — you are a snake charmer. Your hands can make a graceful snake. Is there any other kind?

USE the broom to do a witchy dance. Or a sweep-the-porch dance.

A Little Music, Please

BRING some friends in to move with music.

ASK each friend to bring along a favorite record.

CHOOSE a record and put it on the phonograph. Ask the owner of the record to start moving the way the music makes him feel. Others join him. They may do what he is doing or think up new movements.

GIVE each person a chance to move with his record. Everyone should get to do what each piece of music leads him to do.

TURN OFF the phonograph.

CLAP OUT a rhythm. Ask your friends to walk, hop, or skip in time to your clapping. Let each person clap out a new rhythm to set the others in motion.

PUT some of these movements together to make a dance. Dancing doesn't always need music.

Can anyone do a fandango?

Off the Record

CHOOSE a record that is in good shape.

LISTEN to it over and over. Repeat the words to the song until you know them from memory.

SING the words along with the recording. Be sure to pause where the singer on the recording pauses.

TRY to get into the feeling of the song. Is it sad? happy? romantic? Work out actions and facial expressions that will tell the audience what kind of song you're singing.

PLAY the record again. Go through the motions of singing the song but don't make a sound. Just act like you're singing it. Let the record do the rest.

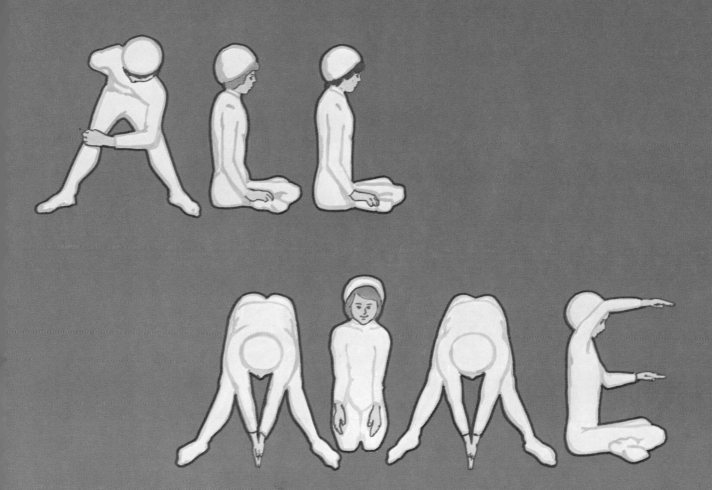

Scents & Nonsense

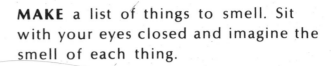

MAKE a list of things to smell. Sit with your eyes closed and imagine the smell of each thing.

BE SURE you smell an onion before you try to smell the next thing on the list. It might be bacon frying or the first spring violet.

INCLUDE things you don't like the smell of, too. How about a skunk or rotten garbage? Concentrate enough and you'll smell it! Phew!

MAKE a list, now, of things you feel with your hands.

CONCENTRATE again. Imagine you are holding an ice cube. Hold it until it feels so cold you can't hold it any more.

PLUNGE your hands into warm water. That feels so good!

CONTINUE down your list.

LIST things to hear.

LISTEN to the clock in the next room. There's not really a clock there. But if you listen with your mind, there will be one. It's a cuckoo clock. Hear it cuckoo six times. Did you hear it? Good.

SIT and listen to silence. Silence is often full of sounds. Sometimes it's even noisy.

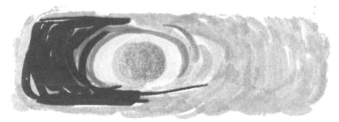

IMAGINE different tastes. Make some sour, sweet, pleasant, bad. You must imagine them so well that your mouth will begin to water.

KEEP your eyes closed and see red. See it very bright and hot. See yellow, feel the yellow of the sun. Now experience the coolness of blue.

TRY to form pictures in your mind's eye of any things you have seen. See a kite in the sky, mountains, or new puppies.

This is the world of imagination. This is the world of pantomime.

Change Is Strange

BE a caterpillar, all fuzzy and lumpy.

CRAWL OUT on a branch. Have you ever noticed how a caterpillar moves?

CHEW on some leaves. Now you are full and feel sleepy.

HOOK the end of your body to the branch. Swing and sway with only the top of your body. Your feet stay in one spot.

FEEL the cool fall wind. It's chilly!

BEGIN to wrap yourself in your warmest threads. Be sure to keep all of your legs tucked in. How about your antennae?

FINISH your sleeping bag cocoon.

BECOME still. Don't move a muscle.

WAIT.

BEGIN to move slowly within your cocoon. The cocoon splits. Part of you pushes out.

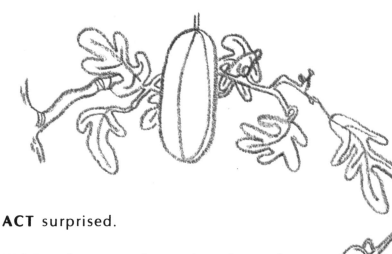

ACT surprised.

WORK the rest of you free from the cocoon. Whew! Hard work!

SHOW that you feel strange. Move your shoulders; wiggle your head. Are you all there? There's something extra.

UNFOLD your arms slowly. With a pumping motion help them to spread out in full wing.

FLUTTER your wings. Experiment with them as though they are a new toy. Then fly away.

When something, like a caterpillar, changes into something else, like a butterfly, that is called metamorphosis. Think of other things that change — seeds that grow into plants or tadpoles that become frogs. Or even frogs that become princes. How would you pantomime that?

Silence Is Golden

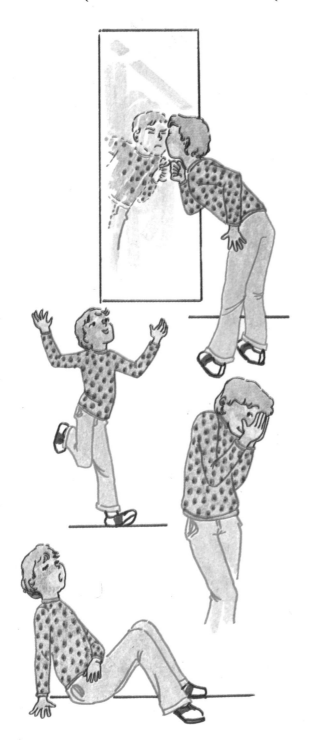

BE QUIET.

DON'T say a word. Your face, hands, and body gestures have to tell the whole story. That is pantomime.

LOOK in a long mirror.

BE ANGRY: scowl, shake your fist.

BE HAPPY: leap, dance, laugh.

BE AFRAID: shrink back, cover your eyes.

BE TIRED: droop your shoulders, yawn.

TRY all kinds of expressions. Use your whole body to get the idea across. Then try putting some together to tell a story.

START OUT being happy. You come across an imaginary box. You are curious, then suspicious.

OPEN it cautiously.

JUMP AWAY in fear because it contains???

Pass It On

SEND four players out of the room. The rest of you decide what to have the four act out.

ASK one of the four to come back into the room. Have a member of the group act out the pantomime you chose.

ASK a second one of the four to come back into the room. She watches the first player act out the pantomime. She mustn't say a word.

ASK the third player to come back into the room. The second player mimics the pantomime for the third. The third only watches. He too, must not say a word.

BRING the last of the four players back into the room. He watches while the third player acts out the pantomime this time.

HAVE the fourth player act out what he thinks the pantomime is.

LET the first pantomimist act it out again. Notice how much it changed.

Got the Picture?

IMAGINE that you are going to take a group picture of the local youth club.

PLACE an empty picture frame on a chair facing the audience. This is an imaginary mirror. Here the characters check how they look before their picture is taken.

ASK several friends to act as the club members. You could act out all of the parts if you are very clever.

HAVE each one look in the imaginary mirror before joining the group to be photographed.

HAVE one girl pretend to put on make-up: lipstick, mascara, rouge.

HAVE a fellow stop and look very hard at himself. He finally removes his dark glasses and looks again. He is scared by what he sees. He quickly puts the glasses back on.

HAVE a boy scowl as he looks in the mirror. He messes up his hair with both hands. He smiles. Now he's satisfied with the way he looks.

HAVE an athletic type guy saunter up to the mirror. He flexes his muscles, sticks out his chest, and looks pleased with himself.

HAVE a girl stop to comb her hair. It's very long so she has to comb and comb and comb. She hits so many snarls and tangles that she takes out a pair of scissors and cuts if off.

LINE UP all the club members.

FOCUS on the group with your camera. Get everyone to smile.

STOP to rearrange people.

GET READY again. Smile. Click.

LOOK at the camera, then at the group. You forgot the film!

How many other characters can you think of to have in the picture?

Guess Again

PLAY this pantomime game with several friends.

DIVIDE into two teams.

HAVE one team act out something like getting up in the morning, cooking a meal, or trying to find a mate for a sock.

TRY TO GUESS what they are doing. When you do, it is your team's turn to pantomime.

TAKE TURNS pantomiming and guessing.

THINK UP other groups of things to act out, such as: fairy tales, what you want to be when you grow up, sports, or songs.

INDEX

Acting Alone, 6
Acting Up, 5-20
Acting Workshop, 18-19
A Little Music Please, 34
An Awful Muddle, 14
animal parade, 14
Change Is Strange, 40
costumes, play, 20
creeping race, 23
dances, 34
Echoes, 10
Get Loose, 22
Got the Picture?, 44
Grab Box, 32
Guess Again, 46
guessing game, 9
I Can't Hear You, 16
imitating voices, 10
Kitchen Action, 28
Mime, 37-46
mini plays, 20
mirror exercises, 6
More than One, 8
Move It, 21-36
ocean animals, 26-27
Ocean Motion, 26-27
Off the Record, 37
pantomime, 8, 9, 37-46
Pass It On, 43
plays for practice, 18-20
Scents and Nonsense, 38
scissor steps, 30
senses (exercise of), 38
Shadows, 11
Shake Down, 24
Silence Is Golden, 42
Silly Situations, 12
slow motion, 26
Springs and Things, 30
"Sylvester and the
   Magic Pebble", 19
swimming make-believe, 12
telephone game, 16
vocal games, 16-17
Walk-About, 25

ILLUSTRATORS

ACTING UP
page   5:   Thomas Petiet
page   6-20: Elizabeth MacGregor

MOVE IT
page   21:   Thomas Petiet
page 22-35:   David LaVerne Laetz
page   36:   Amy Hill

ALL MIME
page   37:   Thomas Petiet
page 38-46:   Amy Hill

About the Editors

   Cameron John and Margaret A. Yerian have advanced degrees in psychology and mass communications from the University of Michigan. They have been active in educational and instructional writing for both adults and children, with many publications to their credit. Their work has ranged from the Educational Television Project in American Samoa, where Mrs. Yerian served as a producer/director and Mr. Yerian was a writer and editor to their present work as media consultants in the Detroit metropolitan area.

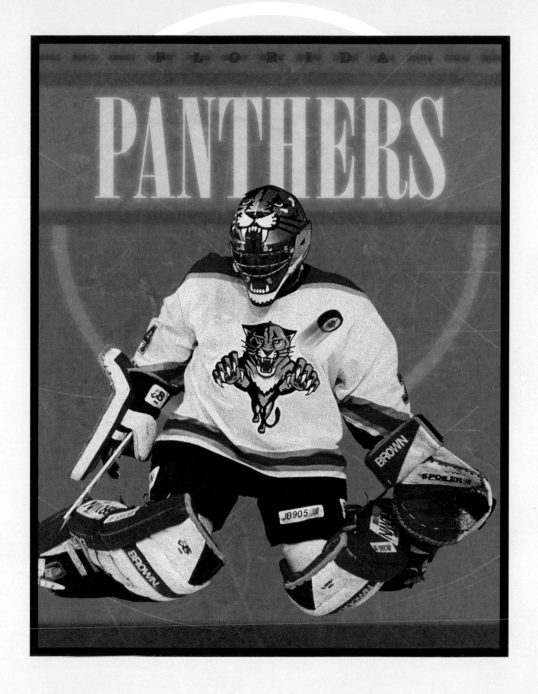

FLORIDA
PANTHERS

JEFF BABINEAU

Published by Creative Education
123 South Broad Street, Mankato, Minnesota 56001
Creative Education is an imprint of The Creative Company

Designed by Rita Marshall
Cover Illustration by Rob Day

Photos by: Bruce Bennett Studios

Library of Congress Cataloging-in-Publication Data

Babineau, Jeff.
Florida Panthers / Jeff Babineau.
p. cm. — (NHL Today)
ISBN 0-88682-738-8

1. Florida Panthers (Hockey team)—History—Juvenile literature.
2. National Hockey League—Juvenile literature. [1. Florida Panthers
(Hockey team)—History. 2. Hockey—History.]
I. Title. II. Series.

GV848.F6B33   1995   94-46767
796.962'64'09759—dc20

123456

INSTANT RIVALRY: JUST ADD FROZEN WATER

The essence, the very sparkle of the night, was unbelievable. That much he knew. But Bill Torrey, president of the expansion Florida Panthers hockey club and the man who had built the New York Islanders into an NHL power in the late 1970s and early 1980s, was finding it difficult to pinpoint the precise reason why.

Was it because the atmosphere at the ThunderDome in St. Petersburg that October evening of 1993 was at a playoff-level pitch? Or did his hard-to-hide emotions stem from the fact that

Scott Levins scored a goal in the Panthers' first win.

27,227 fans—the largest crowd ever to witness a National Hockey League game—had gathered to watch two teams playing ice hockey in Florida?

"To think that 27,000-odd fans would gather inside a building in Florida to watch two expansion teams play . . . I think it's an indication that our game is beginning to gain some ground," Torrey said. "It was a milestone for our league. And the building was so electric that night, it was unbelievable. I'll never forget it. It was almost like a Stanley Cup game or something."

Roger Neilson was named coach and led the Panthers to a 33-34-17 record their first year.

This wasn't the playoffs. And certainly this wasn't an end to anything. For the Panthers, this was the very beginning. Just three games into their NHL existence, the Florida Panthers, a team based in sunny Miami, had already found a heated rival in the upstate Tampa Bay Lightning.

Scott Levins, a 24-year-old right winger who would play 12 games for the Panthers in their inaugural season, scored the only goal the Panthers would need that night, and Tom Fitzgerald iced the game in the final minute by adding an empty-net goal after the Lightning had pulled their goaltender for an extra offensive attacker. Panthers goaltender John Vanbiesbrouck, who was on the cusp of a magical season, made the lead stand up, making 35 saves in recording his first shutout as a Panther, the 17th of his 11-season NHL career.

The Panthers had their first triumph, 2-0, and they couldn't have handpicked a better opponent. Earlier, Tampa Bay's highly vocal president, NHL Hall-of-Famer Phil Esposito, had confidently predicted a victory for his team in front of what he knew would be an NHL record crowd. He went as far as to call the Panthers "pussycats," a shot the Panthers players and management did not find very humorous in the days leading to the game.

Stu Barnes recorded many personal bests in 1993-94 (page 7).

If Esposito was trying to jump-start a rivalry, he was doing a terrific job of it.

Torrey knows a thing or two about good rivalries, too. His New York Islanders had always played competitive games with teams in their division such as Philadelphia and Washington. But when the New York Rangers came to town, there always was a little more on the line, an extra surge of electricity.

"When you have teams that close geographically, I think you have the makings for a good rivalry, no question about that," Torrey said. "It will be a good rivalry, one that is only going to get better with time. It's only natural it will step up a little each year. Hey, we want to be Florida's No. 1 hockey team."

The Panthers proved something that night at the ThunderDome in their 2-0 victory. Despite being a first-year club, they were a team that others could not afford to take lightly.

Team owner H. Wayne Huizenga liked what he saw of his new team that night. The victory gave him special reason to smile.

"They're not going to call us pussycats anymore," he said.

Jody Hull's first goal with the Panthers marked his 100th career point.

A BLUE-LINE BLUEPRINT: THE CONSTRUCTION BEGINS

Building an expansion hockey team is a little like shopping for a car with only $1,000 in your pocket: You're not going to get the pick of the lot, that's for sure. But if you do your homework and kick the tires enough, maybe you can find a model or two that still runs pretty good, and, with a little tinkering under the hood, can give you good performance on the road for years to come.

This was the task the Panthers faced as they hurriedly tried to prepare for the 1993–94 NHL season. The Panthers had been awarded a franchise in December of 1992 along with the Mighty

Ducks of Anaheim (California), and had the option of either joining their new NHL brethren in the fall of 1993 or taking an extra year to prepare, joining for the 1994–95 season.

For the most part, the Panthers had been waiting to see what Anaheim was going to do. So when Anaheim quickly put together a deal to play in a new facility—aptly named The Pond— in time for the 1993–94 season, Florida decided it, too, was ready to immediately jump into the NHL. There would be no waiting. It was April already, and training camp was less than five months away. Everything had to be pieced together at meteor speed.

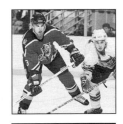

Paul Laus was the Panthers' second defenseman chosen in the 1993 NHL Expansion Draft.

The road ahead was not easy, but the Panthers had several factors working in their favor. In president Bill Torrey and general manager Bob Clarke, the Panthers had two highly knowledgeable hockey men who were familiar with the talent in the league. And just as important as the on-ice decisions that were to be made were the business decisions that needed to be made off the ice. Much of this burden was placed on the shoulders of Dean Jordan, vice president of business and marketing, who had spent the previous year marketing baseball's expansion Florida Marlins. The Panthers' fully assembled staff, pieced together by mid-July, typically was working 14 to 16 hours a day, seven days a week.

"You have the hockey side and the business side, and the thing you have to put together quickest is the business side," Torrey said. "Naming the team, choosing uniforms . . . there are so many things to decide that many people probably overlook. When the Ducks made their deal and told the league they were ready to play, in a matter of 10 days, we had to start to get ready. We wanted to play right away, of course."

Bob Kudelski played in the All-Star Game in 1994 (pages 10-11).

9

Torrey and Clarke locked themselves in a room and began to scour the reserve roster lists of current teams to get an idea of the talent that would be made available to them in the NHL expansion draft in June. Unlike the previous expansion draft, this year NHL teams would be able to protect only one goaltender from the expansion draft, not two. So two items immediately were apparent as Torrey and Clarke began the process of putting a team together: The Panthers likely were going to acquire good goaltending, and they also were likely to get some good, solid players whose strength was on their own end of the ice—the defensive end. The combination would work well under the defensive-minded system of Panthers coach Roger Neilson.

"There were no 40- or 50-goal scorers out there, so when it came down to deciding between Player A and Player B, we looked

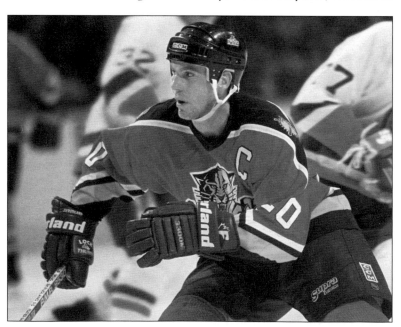

at a player's character and competitiveness," Torrey said. "In our drafting, we rated those qualities very high."

In June, the Panthers unveiled their uniforms for the first time. The team colors were navy blue, red and yellow-gold, and the logo emblazoned on the chest depicted a panther lunging forward, as if in a mode of attack. The Panthers backed their choice of mascots by teaming with the Florida Fish and Wildlife Foundation in a corporate fund-raising program that would raise money to help the Florida panther, a beautiful animal that is facing extinction.

The uniforms, like the panther itself, were breathtaking. All the team had to do now was find some players to fill them.

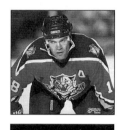

Left wing Mike Hough registered 30 points in his first season as a Panther.

ASSEMBLING THE ON-ICE CAST

The 1993 expansion draft was held in Quebec City, Quebec, in June, and allowed both the Panthers and Mighty Ducks to stock their respective rosters with 24 players. Among the players Florida selected were:

• John Vanbiesbrouck, a former goaltending standout from the New York Rangers who was considered the gem of the expansion draft. Torrey won a coin toss to pick first over Anaheim, and Vanbiesbrouck was his prize.

• Calgary's Brian Skrudland, a former member of the Montreal Canadiens who never had scored many goals, but nonetheless was always a key ingredient on the teams for whom he played. He would become the Panthers' first captain.

• Defenseman Gord Murphy from Boston, whose production had fallen off after he had started his NHL career strongly in Philadelphia.

• Right winger Scott Mellanby of Edmonton, who was coming off a lackluster season with the Oilers after having scored 20 or more goals in four of his previous five seasons. He would lead the Panthers in scoring with 30 goals.

Mike Foligno scored his first goal as a Panther December 8, 1993, against Los Angeles.

What the Panthers lacked in offensive talent they would more than replace with desire and diligence. In the NHL, one of the terms for a hardworking player is a "mucker," and year-in and year-out, such players prove that heart can take a player a long way.

"This team will be different than a lot of other expansion teams," Skrudland told the *Sun-Sentinel* before the season began. "Usually you look up and down the roster of an expansion team and you don't know anyone. But here you've got guys who have been around, guys who have a reputation as 'pains.' They are good, tough players."

Added Clarke, "We don't want teams coming to South Florida like it's some type of a vacation. We want to make this a difficult trip. We want a physical, aggressive team with a strong defense."

These were players other teams had decided, for one reason or another, that they could survive without. And nothing can band together a group of professional athletes faster than when others doubt their ability and challenge their careers.

"We're going to have to work hard for all 60 minutes every night," Skrudland said. "If we take one shift off, that could be it. Whether we believe it or not, ego goes along with being a professional athlete. We've all given up things, but we're not out to prove ourselves to somebody else or to a team or some other organization. We're out to make believers of ourselves, of our teammates. We're here to make a dream come true."

It wasn't difficult to locate the Panthers' first true star. All one had to do was look between the goalposts. Vanbiesbrouck would

Scott Mellanby was top goalscorer during the first season (page 15).

On October 30,
1993, Dave Lowry
scored the Panthers'
first overtime goal,
giving Florida the
victory.

perform well enough to garner strong consideration as the league's most valuable player, and eventually was named as one of three finalists, quite an honor. He finished the season with a goals-against average of 2.53 goals per game, fourth best in the league, and was the winning goaltender of record at the All-Star Game at Madison Square Garden, yet another special moment. "The Beezer," as he is known, faced 40 or more shots 11 times, allowed two or fewer goals in 29 of his 57 decisions, and allowed three or more goals in only 14 of his starts.

"Roger gave John the first shot in goal, and he came out real strong," Torrey said. "Our team checked really hard and played hard defensively, and that really helps our goaltenders. One thing we didn't do was give teams many opportunities."

When they did, when they showed a slight defensive flaw, Vanbiesbrouck often was there to rectify the situation. Said team-

Gord Murphy led the defensemen in scoring in 1993-94.

Brent Severyn is one of the NHL's strongest players.

mate Dave Lowry of the Beezer, "I didn't realize he was as good as he was, on and off the ice. He was the guy who made us believe."

A PLAYOFF CONTENDER

Florida skated to a fast start, gaining 7 points—2 wins, 3 ties—in its first seven games. In the team's season opener in Chicago, the Panthers twice climbed back from deficits in the third period, notching three goals in earning a hard-fought 4-4 tie at Chicago Stadium. Scott Mellanby had the distinction of scoring the first goal in Panthers' history, poking a loose puck past Chicago goaltender Eddie Belfour at the 12:31 mark of the first period. Skrudland scored to give Florida a 4-3 lead in the third period, but Chicago's Jeremy Roenick, a perennial NHL All-Star, notched the tying goal with less than 4 minutes left in regulation. The Panthers settled for a hard-earned tie.

"Anytime you get a point on the road, in a building like this against a team like this, it's a victory for any team, not just an expansion team," defenseman Gord Murphy told the *Sun-Sentinel.* Added Clarke, "We threw fear into them."

Three nights later, the team earned its very first victory against Tampa Bay on the road, and the Panthers nearly won their home opener, too, dropping a tough 2-1 decision to Pittsburgh in front of a sellout crowd of 14,372 at Miami Arena on October 12. The team returned to its winning ways in its fifth game, when rookie Rob Niedermayer, the team's first overall selection in the 1993 NHL entry draft, scored the game winner in a 5-1 triumph. On the same night, Scott Levins became the first Panthers player to score two goals in a game.

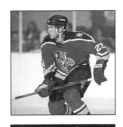

After three months with the team, Scott Levins was traded to Ottawa.

Win or lose, Florida was in close games nearly every night due to the steady play of Vanbiesbrouck and his backup, former New York Islander Mark Fitzpatrick. All but eight of the team's games in the 1993–94 season would be decided by two goals or fewer.

Florida's first road trip through Canada, in November, produced impressive results. After losing to Toronto at Maple Leaf Gardens, the Panthers defeated Quebec, Montreal and Ottawa in a span of five nights. The win against Montreal in the famed Montreal Forum was an accomplishment that was especially meaningful. No franchise in professional sports boasts more championships than the Canadiens, and the Forum's deep tradition means a great deal to members of the NHL fortunate enough to play there. Center Jesse Belanger, a product of Montreal's system, scored the game-winner in a 3-1 victory as the Panthers dominated Montreal, outshooting them by a margin of 38-20.

"This is a special moment," Skrudland would tell his Panthers teammates in the celebration afterward. "Remember it."

Mark Fitzpatrick's 2.73 GAA ranked eleventh in the NHL.

By December, the Panthers really began to pick up steam. Vanbiesbrouck was in net for an emotional 3-2 victory over his old team, the Rangers, who had arrived in Miami riding a 15-game unbeaten streak. It also jump-started an impressive four-game winning streak for the Panthers. And, by the New Year, those pesky, stubborn Panthers were right in the middle of a chase for a playoff spot.

Keith Brown was the Panthers' nominee for the 1994 NHL Masterton Trophy for dedication to hockey.

Many believed the Panthers might soon fall out of the race near midseason, as Tampa Bay had a year earlier after a fast start. By midseason, good teams start building momentum for the play-offs, and lesser teams are left by the wayside. But the Panthers refused to back down. And beginning on January 8 with a game at the Boston Garden, the Panthers embarked on a nine-game

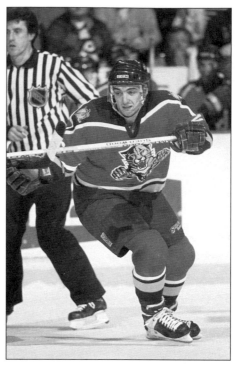

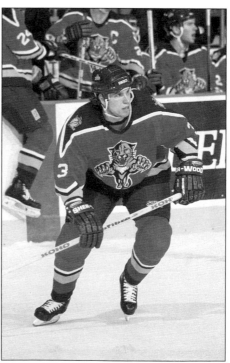

Left to right: Mike Hough, Jesse Belanger, Andrei Lomakin, Paul Laus.

unbeaten string (5-0-4), setting a new standard for an NHL expansion team.

The teams falling to the Panthers—or tying them, at best—were no weaklings, either. Florida tied Pittsburgh, beat Montreal again (5-2) at the Forum, and held the Islanders and Washington Capitals to a goal apiece in consecutive victories. On January 24, Montreal arrived in Miami for a measure of revenge, and the Panthers erupted for eight goals and an 8-3 triumph, with Mellanby and Andrei Lomakin scoring two goals apiece. The incredible streak would continue in overtime deadlocks with Tampa Bay (1-1) and San Jose (3-3), as well as a 3-2 victory over Buffalo. If anybody was under the impression Florida's early success had been a fluke, they couldn't help but believe the Panthers were for real by the arrival of February. The team was 21-17-10, and believing.

Bob Kudelski tied an NHL record for most games played in a season with 86.

"I think what you have is a bunch of guys who set pretty high goals for themselves at the start of the year," Gord Murphy told the *Sun-Sentinel*.

A mid-February stretch in which Florida dropped eight of nine games returned the Panthers to earth, but they still were hovering slightly above the magical .500 plateau, even through March, and still in the thick of the playoff race as the season spilled into April.

Torrey points to April 5 and the Panthers' 80th game—a 3-3 tie with Quebec—as the pivotal date that would decide Florida's fate in its quest for a playoff berth. Florida was ahead 3-1 in the third period and dominating play, but the Nordiques rallied to tie the game and steal a point. Meanwhile, the New York Islanders ended up scoring a late third-period goal and tacking on another in overtime that night to pick up a point on Florida in the stand-

John Vanbiesbrouck is one of the league's MVPs (pages 26-27).

Tom Fitzgerald led the team with three shorthanded and three empty net goals.

ings. On April 12, the second-to-last game of the regular season, the Nordiques officially knocked Florida from the playoffs with a 5-2 win at Miami Arena.

Florida had fallen short of its goal—the team staggered at the finish, winning only once in nine games—but still, players had plenty of reason to be proud of their season. The team had established NHL first-year team records for most points (83), most victories (33, tied with Anaheim), most road victories (18), and longest unbeaten streak (nine games). An emotional 4-1 home victory over the Islanders on April 14 in the season finale—a sellout crowd's appreciative standing ovation moved team owner H. Wayne Huizenga to tears—left the Panthers just one game shy of finishing .500 for the season. Florida finished 33-34-17, one point removed from the eighth and final playoff spot in the NHL's Eastern Conference.

"I think people had the feeling that expansion teams never made the playoffs," Skrudland told the *Sun-Sentinel.* "But I doubt there've been many expansion teams with goalies who were up for a major award [as was John Vanbiesbrouck, for MVP]. That in itself is a big thing, but add to that the fact we're the third or fourth best defensive team in the league. If you would have said that about an expansion team at the beginning of the year, they would have laughed in your face."

Added Torrey, "Nobody is all-seeing, but I had a sense early on that this team was going to be one that would hang tough throughout the season. We did."

As players went their different ways for the offseason, most did so with many fond memories. Said goaltender Mark Fitzpatrick to the *Sun-Sentinel,* "The one thing I'll always remember is the heart

Andrei Lomakin is a top scorer for the team.   29

Bill Lindsay plays aggressive hockey.

of my teammates. I never played for a bunch of guys with so much heart. That's the biggest thing I'll leave this season with."

For Torrey, Clarke, Neilson and all the Panthers, it had been quite an incredible journey. The team had made significant inroads in Miami, a land previously a stranger to the sport of hockey. The Panthers produced clinics in Little Havana and had their games broadcast by radio in Spanish as well as English. Traditionally a game of the frozen North, hockey was at home in the Sunshine State.

But even Torrey found it a little unusual when, during training camp, he arrived at the rink with the outside temperatures climbing to 95 degrees.

"It's so hot and humid outside, and we're inside the rink, looking at hockey players," Torrey said. "That seemed pretty strange. But you know, it really doesn't matter: Whether you're in Flin Flon, Canada, or Fort Lauderdale, Florida, a rink is a rink."

Rookie Rob Niedermayer is a top playmaker, adding 17 assists in 1993-94.

Anaheim Mighty Ducks
Buffalo Sabres
Boston Bruins
Calgary Flames
Chicago Blackhawks
Dallas Stars
Detroit Red Wings
Edmonton Oilers
Florida Panthers
Hartford Whalers
Los Angeles Kings
Montreal Canadiens
New Jersey Devils
New York Islanders
New York Rangers
Ottawa Senators
Pittsburgh Penguins
Philadelphia Flyers
St. Louis Blues
San Jose Sharks
Tampa Bay Lightning
Toronto Maple Leafs
Vancouver Canucks
Washington Capitals
Winnipeg Jets